TOUGH GUIDES

HOW TO SURVIVE ON A
DESERT ISLAND

JIM PIPE

WAYLAND
www.waylandbooks.co.uk

First published in Great Britain in 2018 by Wayland
Copyright © Hodder & Stoughton, 2018.
All rights reserved.

Produced for Wayland by Calcium Creative Ltd
Editors: Sarah Eason and Jennifer Sanderson
UK Editor: Sarah Ridley
Designer: Simon Borrough
Cover design: Cathryn Gilbert

ISBN: 978 1 5263 0962 4
10 9 8 7 6 5 4 3 2 1

Wayland, an imprint of
Hachette Children's Group
Part of Hodder and Stoughton
Carmelite House
50 Victoria Embankment
London EC4Y 0DZ

An Hachette UK Company
www.hachette.co.uk
www.hachettechildrens.co.uk

Printed and bound in China

MIX
Paper from
responsible sources
FSC® C104740
FSC
www.fsc.org

Photo Credits: Cover: Shutterstock: Eduard Kyslynskyy, Vlad Ghiea. Inside: Steve F-E Cameron
(Merlin-UK) 27tl; Shutterstock: Annetje 5tl, ArtTomCat 4c, Brocreative 24c, Kris Butler 13t,
Jakub Cejpek 11c, Bobby Deal/RealDealPhoto 17tl, Dirk Ercken 10br, EcoPrint 22cl, FotoVeto
19t, Paolo Gianti 4l, 16l, lkunl 25t, Iakov Kalinin 23t, Intraclique LLC 15c, Xavier Marchant 6l, 18l,
Mayskyphoto 29t, Movit 8l, 20l, Tyler Olson 8cl, PhotoHappiness 4cr, Pinosub 6c, Leigh Prather
26cl, Daniel Rajszczak 16c, Valery Shanin 28cl, Szefei 7c, Aleksandar Todorovic 18cl, Graham
Tomlin 14c, Andrij Vatsyk 9t, Dani Vincek 12l, 24l, Vladoskan 14l, 26l, VVO 10l, 22l, Marty Wakat
21c, Richard Waters 20c, David Wingate 12c.

Contents

SURVIVAL!

Thanks to planes, our world is getting smaller. We can fly across a huge ocean in a few hours. Yet many parts of our planet are still wild and dangerous. Sometimes a fierce storm can send a ship crashing into the rocks, or a faulty engine can force a plane to land in the ocean.

Pacific Ocean

PACIFIC OCEAN
WHERE: stretches from Australia and Asia to the Americas
AREA: 155 million square kilometres

desert island

Imagine surviving a plane crash or **shipwreck**. You struggle ashore, only to find yourself all alone on a deserted island. You are in the middle of the Pacific Ocean, thousands of kilometres from the nearest town. Suddenly, the world seems very, very big. Could you survive? How might you be rescued?

I SURVIVED

In 1722, sailor Philip Ashton hid on a desert island after escaping from pirates. At first he lived on nothing but fruit. Then by chance, he met an English **castaway**. The man vanished into the jungle three days later. Luckily, he left behind several knives. Using these, Ashton could hunt tortoises for food. He was rescued by a ship soon after.

DESERT ISLAND

WHERE: often **tropical** but found all over the world

LARGEST: Devon Island, off northern Canada: 55,247 square kilometres

SURVIVING THE SURF

If your ship is sinking, you need to act quickly. Gather as much food and water as you can. If you do not have a life raft or **life jacket**, cling to something large that floats by. Kick slowly towards the island. Listen for the roar of the surf. The waves can push you to shore. Watch out for razor-sharp **coral reefs** below the surface. They rip skin to shreds.

coral reef

CORAL REEF
WHERE: usually found along tropical coastlines
LARGEST: Great Barrier Reef, Australia: 2,575 km long

I SURVIVED

In 1943, a US navy boat was sunk by a Japanese destroyer. Braving sharks and crocodiles, the survivors swam to a nearby island. After two days without food and water, they swam to a bigger island. For six days, they survived on coconuts before being rescued. One of the survivors was John F Kennedy, who later became the President of the United States.

If you make it to land, your chances of survival are much higher. It is easier to stay alive on an island than adrift at sea. If you take the right steps, you can build a **shelter**, find food and water, and make a fire for warmth, cooking and protection.

waterfall

WATERFALL
USE: perfect for washing yourself and your clothing
THREAT: a sudden gush of water can sweep you away

OVER HERE!

If you are very lucky, you might find there are people already on the island. However, in the Pacific Ocean there are more than 30,000 islands and most have no one living on them. That is why they are called desert, or deserted, islands. You will need to do your best to attract attention and, hopefully, someone will rescue you.

SOS help signal

SOS DISTRESS SIGNAL
USE: international distress signal that is easy to type in **Morse code:** · · · — — — · · ·
THREAT: if written on a beach, watch for high tides

fire signal

Shipping lanes criss-cross the oceans. Passing ships and planes will probably pass your island at some point. The problem is letting rescuers know where you are. A smoky fire is the best way to attract attention. Build it on top of a hill or cliff, so that it can be seen from a long way away.

TOUGH TIP

Use seaweed, rocks or branches to spell out a message such as SOS or HELP. Leave your message in an open area. You can also use one of these well-known codes:

V = need help
X = need medical help
↑ = head this way

FIRE SIGNAL
INTERNATIONAL DISTRESS SIGNAL: three fires in a triangle
ADVANTAGE: easy to see from aircraft

LIGHTING A FIRE

A fire has many uses: as a signal, for cooking and for light and warmth at night. The smoke also keeps insects away. To start a fire you need a material that catches light easily, called **tinder**. The fibres from palm tree trunks work well. On top of the tinder, place the **kindling**. Then put lots of dead, dry palm leaves on top.

palm tree

PALM TREE
USE: green palm leaves create thick, white smoke when burned

TOUGH TIP

You can create fire by rubbing one piece of wood very fast against another. The wood gets very hot and sets the tinder on fire. Be warned. This is not very easy and takes a lot of skill and practice.

If you do not have matches or lighters, set fire to tinder by focusing the Sun's hot rays on it with a pair of glasses. Even the shiny bottom of a drinks can might work! Practise until you can light your signal fire quickly, in case you see a ship or plane passing by.

fire-making skills

FIRE-MAKING SKILLS
NEEDED: tinder, kindling, hard wooden stick, piece of soft wood
ACTION: spin hard wooden stick to create a flame

WASHED UP

After a shipwreck, the remains of the ship and its **cargo** often get washed ashore. Look around the island for any washed-up objects. Look out for items such as matches, a knife, a **compass**, a lighter and a **first-aid kit**. If your life raft has survived the trip ashore, you can use it as a shelter.

life raft

LIFE RAFT

WHAT: a boat used to get to safety

USE: often kitted out with drinking water, food packets, a fishing kit, a mirror, flares and a first-aid kit

survival essentials

Almost all cargo has some use. A plastic bag or bottle can be used to carry or store water. A short length of rope can help you trap animals or build a raft. A piece of wire can be bent and used to make a fish hook to catch fish.

TOUGH TIP

Dental floss can be used to make a clothes line or shoelaces, or to use as thread to mend holes in your clothes.

SURVIVAL ESSENTIALS

WHAT: matches, compass and knife
USE: matches to start a fire, compass to find your way, knife to cut and hunt

MAKING A SHELTER

Unless you come across a suitable cave, you will need to build your own shelter. First, find your materials. Bamboo is light and strong and perfect for making a frame. Palm leaves provide excellent cover. Start with a simple **lean-to**. Plant two Y-shaped branches in the sand about 1.8 m apart. Take a long branch and place it between the forks. This creates a **ridge pole**.

driftwood

DRIFTWOOD
WHAT: wood washed ashore
USE: fire, shelter or boat building

Lean more sticks or bamboo poles against the ridge pole to form a roof. Tie everything together with vines. You can also use lengths of bark from a hibiscus tree. It peels off like string. Place layers of palm leaves over your frame. To keep warm at night, line the floor with more palm leaves.

shelter

SHELTER
MADE FROM: driftwood
USE: protects from the Sun, wind, rain and some animals

ANIMAL DANGER

Tropical islands may look like paradise, but they are home to some deadly creatures. Spiders and scorpions can give very serious bites. Though snakes are common on Pacific islands, only a few can harm you. If you do come across a snake, keep your distance. Crocodiles are a lot more dangerous. They are very fast over short distances, even out of water.

crocodile

CROCODILE
SIZE: grows up to 6 m long
THREAT: fast on land and in the water, powerful jaws and sharp teeth

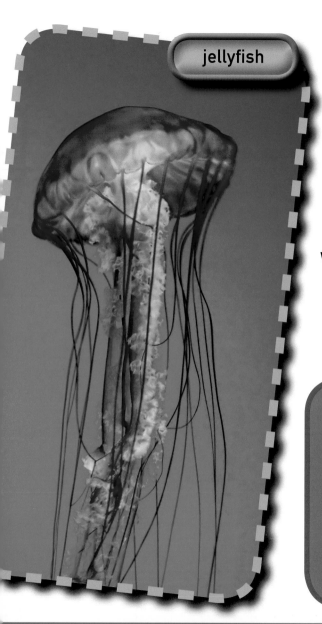

jellyfish

Watch out for box jellyfish. They have a very painful sting. Komodo dragons can grow up to 3 m long. These giant lizards have a bite so poisonous it can kill you. Even more deadly is the tiny cone snail. A drop of its poison can kill 20 people. Wear shoes, even in water.

TOUGH TIP

Tiger sharks are known to attack humans near to the shore. Remember, they are most active at dawn and dusk. Get out of the water if you are bleeding because blood can attract sharks.

JELLYFISH
SWARM: up to 100,000 jellyfish in a large bloom (group)
THREATS: many have a painful sting

FOOD AND WATER

You can live for two weeks without food but only three to four days without water. If you cannot find a stream, use large leaves to **funnel** rainwater into empty coconut shells. The next best thing is to drink coconut milk. Climb the tree and twist the nut until it breaks free.

coconut tree

TOUGH TIP

Never stand under a coconut tree and shake it to get coconuts. Every year people die from coconuts landing on their head!

COCONUT TREE
SIZE: up to 30 m tall
USE: young, green coconuts contain lots of vitamins and minerals

wild pigs

Wild pigs are found on many Pacific islands, but it is a real challenge to catch them. Birds are much easier to catch. Find out where they nest and feed. Then trap them with a **snare** made from a loop of string or a shoelace. Birds' eggs make a great meal although gulls will attack anyone who comes near their nests. Frogs, snakes and some types of large insect can all be eaten, too.

WILD PIGS

USE: food. Skin can be used for clothes.

THREAT: sharp tusks make them very dangerous if threatened

SEAFOOD DINNER

Along with coconuts and fruit, fish are your best bet for a meal. Bend a safety pin to make a fish hook, or sharpen a bamboo stick to make a spear. If you are a good swimmer, try diving underwater. If not, wade into knee-deep water. The water may distort the distance between you and the fish, so aim your throw around 15 cm ahead of your target. Try spearing the fish against a hard surface, such as a rock.

land crab

LAND CRAB
WHERE: found on most tropical islands
USE: meat in crab claws tastes good when cooked

TOUGH TIP

Be warned, poison in some fish can make you ill. Avoid eating jellyfish, fish with spikes or beaks, or those that puff up. If you are desperate for food, you can boil some seaweed to make a healthy soup.

Make yourself an underground oven to cook your catch. Dig yourself a hole in the ground. Then line it with hot rocks heated in your fire. Wrap the fish in palm leaves to keep it clean and moist. Put the wrapped fish on top of the rocks, cover it all with sand and leave it to cook.

filefish

FILEFISH
SIZE: up to 1 m long
USE: can be roasted and eaten

ISLAND WEAR

A tropical island is very hot. This is great for a summer holiday but deadly on a desert island. Even on a cloudy day, the Sun will burn your skin in 15 minutes. Avoid the midday Sun, as **sunstroke** can be a killer. Stay in the shade as much as possible and always cover your head.

Avoid midday Sun.

MIDDAY SUN
TEMPERATURE: 27°C to 32°C
THREAT: Sun beats down for 10 hours or more on tropical islands

palm leaves

Most clothes today are not built for life on a desert island. You will have plenty of time, so learn how to make new clothes from palm leaves and coconut shells.

PALM LEAVES

LENGTH: up to 3.6 m long
USE: leaves can be woven to make baskets, mats, sacks, fans and hats

EXPLORE!

At some point you will probably want to explore your island. You might find a better place to fish or to set up your shelter. But many Pacific islands are rocky and mountainous, and fast-flowing rivers can sweep you off your feet. You can get stuck in swamps and **quicksand**. Leave a trail of pebbles to show the route back to your shelter.

high ground

HIGH GROUND
USE: a good view of your island
THREATS: falling rocks, slippery surfaces, cliffs and smoky volcanoes

fresh water

TOUGH TIP

Watch out for the Sun as you wander around. Rub coconut oil, a natural moisturiser, onto your skin. Even better is the sticky ooze from a mushroom coral. This works like SPF 50 sunblock. Put the coral back in the sea and you can use it again the next day!

If you have a pen and paper, make a map of your island. Mark on it good places to find fresh water, fruit trees or even waterfalls where you can take a shower. Spend a few days on the other side of the island, just in case ships pass by on that side

FRESH WATER
WHERE: in ponds, rivers, lakes, ice, snow and under the ground
THREAT: can contain parasites and diseases

FEELING LONELY

It can get lonely on an island all by yourself. The important thing is to stay calm and think clearly. The ocean may separate you from home but it is likely that a ship will pass by and rescue you. Make plans or scratch a mark on a tree as each day passes to keep up your spirits.

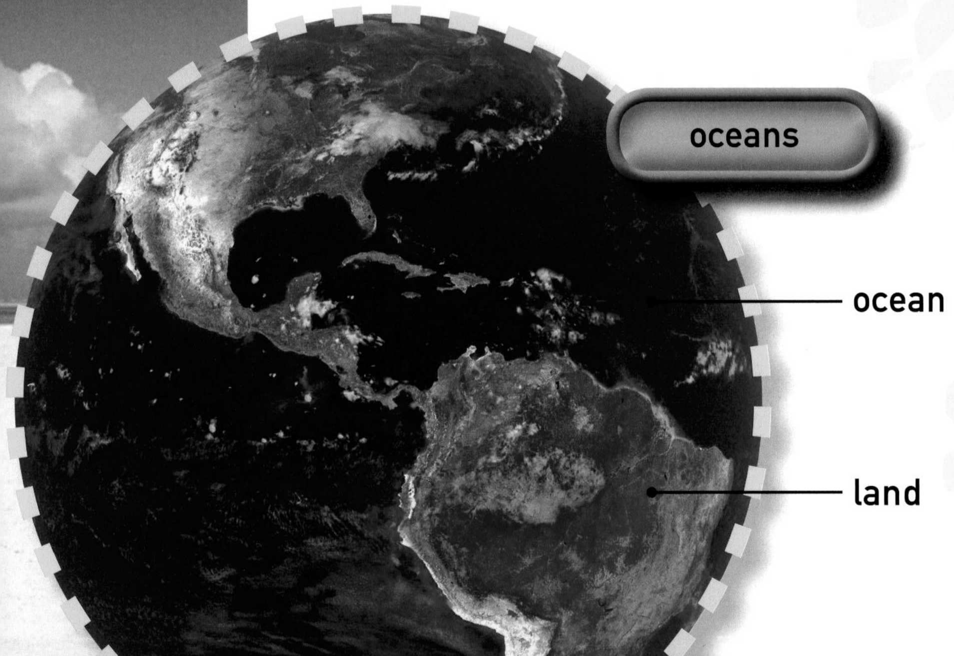

oceans

ocean

land

OCEANS
MAJOR OCEANS: Pacific, Atlantic, Indian, Arctic and Southern
SIZE: 71 per cent of the world is covered by ocean

These days, most castaways are eventually rescued. One man was stranded on an island during the 2004 **tsunami** in the Indian Ocean. He was found 25 days later, waving a flag made from some of his clothes. Even if you are not rescued within a few days, do not give up hope. Help is probably on its way.

Alexander Selkirk

I SURVIVED

In 1704, Scottish sailor Alexander Selkirk was **marooned** on an island in the middle of the Pacific. At first he read his Bible and waited to be rescued. When this did not happen, he made the best of life on the island. He hunted goats for food and built two huts out of wood. Finally, five years later, he was rescued.

ALEXANDER SELKIRK
TOOLS: musket, gunpowder, carpenter's tools, a knife, a Bible, some clothing and rope
THREATS: sea lions, rats and Spanish sailors (his enemies)

RESCUE

Most castaways are faced with a tough choice, to either stay on their island or take their chances on the ocean. Most desert islands have the materials to build a raft. Bamboo is the best material. It is light, strong and floats well. You can make a sail by weaving palm leaves together and tying them to another bamboo frame.

bamboo raft

BAMBOO
SIZE: 14 m long
USES: medicines, shelter, furniture, paper, flutes and fishing rods. Young shoots can be eaten.

rescue helicopter

It can be tough surviving on the ocean. It is usually safer to stay on your island if you have a good supply of food and water. One day a passing ship or aircraft will see the smoke from your signal fire, and you will be rescued. Some survivors have liked their desert island so much they decided to stay!

I SURVIVED

Not all desert islands are tropical. About 500 years ago, a 19-year-old French woman named Marguerite de La Rocque was marooned on an island off the coast of Canada. She survived by hunting wild animals. She lived in a cave for two years until a fishing boat finally rescued her.

RESCUE HELICOPTER
TYPE: Sikorsky HH-60 Pave Hawk
SPEED AND RANGE: 360 km/h; range of 805 km

GLOSSARY

cargo Objects carried by a ship or plane.

castaway Someone who is adrift or shipwrecked.

compass A device that points towards north and can be used to find your way.

coral reef Rock-like structures built by tiny ocean animals.

first-aid kit A box filled with medicines and bandages.

funnel To pour liquid into an object that is wide at one end and narrow at the other.

kindling Material that catches fire easily, such as small, dry sticks of wood, dry grass or tree bark.

lean-to A shelter made by leaning material such as wood against something.

life jacket A jacket filled with air that helps you to float in the water.

marooned Left on a desert island or other uninhabited place.

Morse code Signalling code made of dots and dashes.

quicksand A deep pit filled with sand and water that can suck you in.

ridge pole A long pole across the top of a tent or shelter.

shelter A structure that protects you.

shipwreck When a ship sinks in a storm.

snare A trap.

sunstroke An illness that can kill you, which is caused by too much Sun.

tinder A material that easily bursts into flames.

tropical Hot, wet regions midway between the North and South Poles.

tsunami A giant tidal wave caused by an underwater earthquake.

FURTHER READING

Jinny Johnson. *The Open Ocean (Watery Worlds).*
Franklin Watts, 2015

Richard Spilsbury and Louise Spilsbury. *Shipwrecked! Explore floating and sinking and use science to survive (Science Adventures).*
Franklin Watts, 2017

Susie Brooks, *Where on Earth? Coastlines,*
Wayland, 2015

WEBSITES

Play this survival game on the website of the National Museums, Liverpool:
www.liverpoolmuseums.org.uk/kids/games-quizzes/survival/index.aspx

BBC Nature videos about shallow seas and the wildlife in them:
www.bbc.co.uk/nature/habitats/Neritic_zone

Dreamsworks TV 'Survival Hacks - How to survive on a desert island':
www.youtube.com/watch?v=HfQag78Q4TI

INDEX